YOUR KNOWLEDGE HAS VALUE

- We will publish your bachelor's and master's thesis, essays and papers

- Your own eBook and book - sold worldwide in all relevant shops

- Earn money with each sale

Upload your text at www.GRIN.com
and publish for free

Bibliographic information published by the German National Library:

The German National Library lists this publication in the National Bibliography; detailed bibliographic data are available on the Internet at http://dnb.dnb.de .

This book is copyright material and must not be copied, reproduced, transferred, distributed, leased, licensed or publicly performed or used in any way except as specifically permitted in writing by the publishers, as allowed under the terms and conditions under which it was purchased or as strictly permitted by applicable copyright law. Any unauthorized distribution or use of this text may be a direct infringement of the author s and publisher s rights and those responsible may be liable in law accordingly.

Imprint:

Copyright © 2018 GRIN Verlag
Print and binding: Books on Demand GmbH, Norderstedt Germany
ISBN: 9783668795020

This book at GRIN:

https://www.grin.com/document/441310

Adil Ouatat

Narrate stories through food. About Diana Abu Jaber's novel "Crescent"

GRIN Verlag

GRIN - Your knowledge has value

Since its foundation in 1998, GRIN has specialized in publishing academic texts by students, college teachers and other academics as e-book and printed book. The website www.grin.com is an ideal platform for presenting term papers, final papers, scientific essays, dissertations and specialist books.

Visit us on the internet:

http://www.grin.com/

http://www.facebook.com/grincom

http://www.twitter.com/grin_com

"Without ever realizing it, Camille had fallen under the spell of the Siren's call: the sound that contains of scent of berries, chocolate, and mint, what tastes of salt and oil and blood, that sounds like a heart's murmur, the passage of clouds to prayers, the beloved's name and a distant ringing in the ears". (Jaber, 2004)

Narrate Stories through food:

Diana Abu Jaber in her novel *Crescent* uses food as a complex language to communicate love, memory and exile. Food also is a metaphor by which Abu Jaber questions the symbolic boundaries embodied in culture, closes, and ethnicity. Food is a real conservatory of the homeland memories and gives up the possibility to imagine mingled identities and traditions. In the novel, the food stands to use a metaphor that deals with the presence and absence of cultural and familial bands. Furthermore, food builds the act of narration through the actions which come to pass in kitchens; those actions mark the pain of exile and loss as well as the hope of family and community. To put it differently, the kitchen becomes "first things taste" which refers to be a cupboard or a "shrine" (Shihab, 1995). So, Abu Jaber uses food to build space in which the possibilities of peace, love and community that are imagined. Lisa Suhair Majaj in Arab *American literature and politics of memory* suggests that Nye's poetry "explores the markers of cross cultural complexity" (Majaj, 1996). From this point, Dina Abu Jaber's novel tends to discuss the act of cooking and food. The character Aziz who is a poet quotes "let the beauty we love be what we do, there are hundreds of ways to kneel and kiss the ground" (Jaber, 2004). Carolyn Korsmeyer states that "eating together is a common signal among most peoples for friendship, tierce or celebration" she adds, "Both eating and narrative are cultural practices. When food is treated in fiction therefore, it brings to light the way eating may achieve significance within the tradition the narrative in question addresses or in which it participates" she adds that "the intimacy of eating trust presumed the social equality of those who sit down together, and the shared tastes and pleasures of the table". (Korsmeyer, 1999)

In this vein, food can be analyzed in non-verbal dimension as well as be listed as cultural experience that cannot be readily translated.

Diana's novel *Crescent* uses food as a language through which the characters migrate and live the nostalgia of their home land Identity. Food becomes a sphere of refuge or a contact zone where "the spare of colonial encounters, the space in which peoples geographically and historically separated come into contact with each other and establish ongoing relations" also this contact contains "conditions of coercion, radical inequality, and intractable conflict" (Pratt, 1992), so the contact zone used in the novel seems to be a domestic one that located in cafés, kitchens and homes from this perspectives the novel confirms the theme of the world- as- home and the theme of personal as political.

Moreover, food as a contact language may be employed as one of "improvised language that develop among speakers of different native languages who need to communicate with each other consistently, usually in context of trade" Pratt emphasizes that contact zone "such languages are commonly regarded as chaotic, barbarous, lacking in structure" (Pratt, 1992). Abu Jaber's novel *Crescent* and the memoir *The Language of Baklava*, use food as a bridge which melts the gap that is sounds as aches and add structure to narrative. Diana commits that "eating is one of the things that crystallize your experiences and the metaphor of food is a way to translate these cultural experiences. Thus, the treatment of food in *Crescent* becomes a "safe" way from white American readers to listen to dangerous to picks like war, Iraq, the middle east" (Esa, 2002). Here, the food is used as an act of translation.

One of the major items that Diana tackles in her writings is to humanize the Arabs, "to put a human face on people who are culturally erased" , provide human histories, family life, the day-to- day small things that people can relate to, food, family, love, loss" (Esa, 2002). Diana Abu Jaber in *Crescen*t tries to give more important signs to the storytelling in its relation to food. The novel centers on the way *Serine* makes food as well as her uncle ways of telling story. These two progressions happen and cross each other in the kitchen where *Serine* feeds her uncle the Arabic food, and he tells her the Scherazadian tales. "A lesser- Known fact about jinns (genies)", the uncle explains that their homes may lack "living rooms or dining rooms or studies or bathrooms or even every comfortable beds, they do like a nice kitchen, to satisfy their sweet tooth, may be bake a little knaffea, brew a little coffee, have a few people over- that sort of things" (Jaber, 2004), this extract tries to resemble *Serine* to Jinns as the blond haired, blue eyes chef of Iraqi descent who appreciates a nice kitchen *Serine* utilizes food to become a contact language, to say it differently, a canal to translate experience and bring meaning to the world.

Food is interchangeable to love, prayer and healing as stop was young, Serine uses the contact language and further, she uses it as translation in order to create an understandable communication with the surrounding in the café. Serine learned that "food was better than love: surer, truer, more satisfying and enriching. As long as she could lose herself in the rhythms of peeling an onion, she was complete and whole and as long as she could cook, she would be loved" (Jaber, 2004). From this angle, the only truth that Serine is cooking "the only truth she seemed to possess" (Jaber, 2004) the act of cooking seems to be a strength and force for Serine, when she fails in her life, when she has a feeling of uncertainty confusion and identify conflict, she goes to the kitchen to realize her existence through cooking.

Franz fanon's epigraph "in the world through a travel, I am endlessly creating myself" (Fanon, 1967) which going parallel with the act of cooking; besides characters in Diana's novel constitute hybrid identities that intertwine strength and choice within a fluid and stander space, the characters Tries to situate themselves as Arab, American, or Arab- American.

Abu Jaber tries to discuss the topic of difference through the people and places in order to show that identity is a fluid and often illusory. When Serine asks Aziz if he is Muslim, he shrugs and in an answer, that evokes Walt Whitman, replies, "Who knows? I am Aziz large, I contain multitudes. I defy classification" (Jaber, 2004).The epigraph highlights that we cannot recognize persons from the appearance that he or she shows. As a result, Serine who is Blond, white skinned is a half Arab. The covered Man who kidnaps Abdelrahman is covered woman who transforms to a mermaid Queen Alieph. The police officers go to Nadia's café not to annoy customers and clients, but to look for hummus and to catch up on their favorite Arabic soap operas on TV. To make it more easily, here I notice that identities becomes fluid and slipper through which the characters center around the food.

Homi Bhabha developed a new concepts into colonial discourse in order to challenge the pre-established notions of imperialism, he states "dispels the specter of pure culture with the realism of hybridity" and also "spools the intricate, delectable misunderstanding between the colonize and the colonized with the image of mimicry" and he presents a third space that « quite properly challenges our sense of the historical identity of culture as a homogenizing, unifying force" (Bhabha, 1994). Diana's novel the *Crescent* examines the mentions of cross-culturalism and the being in the in between.

Bhabha states "what is theoretically innovative, and politically crucial, is the need to think beyond narratives of ordinary and initial subjectivities and to focus on those moments or processes that are produced in the articulation of cultural differences" (Bhabha, 1994). So, "in between" spaces "provide the terrain for elaborating strategies of self-hood- singular or communal – that initiate new signs of identity, and innovative sites of collaboration and contestation, in the act of defining the idea of society itself" (Bhabha, 1994).

Self-identity and origins seem to be the central questions that Serine tries to find their answer. Moreover, Serine tries to elaborate techniques of selfhood especially when she looks in the mirror "all she can see is white" and describing her eyes as "almond –shaped, and see green" also other features as "tidy and compact. Entirely her mother" (Jaber, 2004). From those epigraphs, persons wonder as they know that Serine in held Arab. Serine deliberates that she "inherited her mother on the outside and her father from inside, and she thinks of she could examine" the blood and bones and the shape of her mind and emotions- she thinks she would find her truer and deeper nature". She "imagines her parents, young expecting their first child, expecting, perhaps, a true amalgam of their two bodies. Were they disappointed, she wonders, to have an entirely fair-skinned child?" (Jaber, 2004). This statement clarifies Serine's Questions about her origins are in-between as Arab- American.

Serine looks for her identity within this concept of in-between of cultural difference through food and in contradiction of her uncle's stories. As Serine feels loss and exile and as a result to look for her nostalgia and security let her to seek comfort in cooking. Respectively, food is defined as Serine's moods, philosophy of life, and existence in the world. Moreover, Serine gets surprised why "whenever she tries to deliberately seek out something like God, she gets distracted… and she finds that instead she is thinking about something like stuffed grape leaves rolled tightly around rice, ground land, garlic, onions, currants, fragrant with green olive oil"

(Jaber, 2004). Her close thinking is "to exist inside the simplest actions, like chopping an onion or stirring a pot" (Jaber, 2004).

Food stands as a source for exploring identity and legacy. Serine knows cooking from her parents and "even though her mother was American, her (Iraq) father always said his wife thought about food like an Arab" (Jaber, 2004).

The absence of her parents let Serine to utilize food and cooking as the only way to ratify her narratives and origin. She says, "I think food should taste like where it comes from. I mean good food especially". She explains, "You can sort of trace it back. You know, so the best butter tastes a little like pastures and flowers, that sort of stuff things shows their origins" (Jaber, 2004). Majaj advocates this through this epigraph "memory plays a familiar role in the assertion of identity by members of ethnic and minority groups." also she links between memory "remembering who you are" and family narratives respectively, "memory functions on both a cultural and a personal level to establish narratives of origin and belonging, myths of people hood, like memories of childhood situate the subject and make agency possible" (Majaj, 1996).

But Serine was confused about her origin especially when she attends a meeting of women in Islam and when she introduces her name "her heart begins hammering and her mind goes blank… 'Serine', she manages to stay 'I cook'" (Jaber, 2004). From this perspective, the only place which makes Serine purifies her origins and her identity is the kitchen.

Food has other signification, Hanif tries to assimilate American stream as he studies the Joy of cooking and the Betty Crocker cookbook, just to prepare a traditional American meal for Serine. Hanif seemed to "intrigued by the new kind of cooking, a shift of ingredients like a move from native tongue into a foreign language: butter instead of olive; potatoes instead of rice, beef instead of lamb" (Jaber, 2004). Similarly, in *the language of baklava*, Diana Abu Jaber states Aunt Aya words "eating is a form of listening" (Jaber, The Language of Baklava, 2005). Partly, Hanif is a translator of Arabic and English literature, he easily understands the language Serine uses. In reality, as Hanif feeds Serine "a morsel of Lamb from his fingers" it stands as "Food is their own private language" (Jaber, 2004); food is presented as a contact language as well as a semiotic item which will be highlighted later. In a statement, Hanif makes it clear that he likes "the kitchen, the table, stove, where the women were always telling stories" (Jaber, Crescent , 2004). This confession to Serine just to express that Han never want to be on up in his "father's Orchad" (Jaber, Crescent , 2004). The conversation with Serine about old home revives Hanif's memories of both home and country. Lost home is embodied by exile and alienation that the novel *Crescent* represents through displacement of death, politics, or misunderstanding. The concept of alienation is illustrated in the depiction of Hanif as a character who flees from Iraq through the desert. Additionally, Serine also draws our attention to the loss of her parents and how she feels the abandonment of their long absences from home:

> *''[I] t wasn't the same thing as crossing the desert' she says softly 'But in a way what's sort of how it felt waiting for them to come home''* (Jaber, Crescent , 2004).

Similarly, Serine and Hanif experience the ordeal of exile. Serine really understands Han's declaration which "You are the place I want to be- you're the opposite of exile" (Jaber, Crescent , 2004). For this reason, Serine gets afraid of feeding Hanif old dishes just not to wake his cultural identity and belonging to Iraq. Serine does not make the *frekah*. Instead, she prepares a traditional American breakfast of bacon and eggs. In this manner, the food of home is important for persons who live in exile, outside culture of origin and home. Diana Abu Jaber states that *Crescent* investigates the concept of exile as a painful experience for an immigrant. Furthermore, Abu Jaber digs deeply in the consciousness of human mind to mirror the hardships one goes through as an outcast with a lost identity. This is clearly stated in Shalal Esa's so mentioned article:

> "*what a painful thing it is to be an immigrant. How when you leave your home country, you don't really know what it is that's about to happen to you. What an incredible experience and journey it is. And how for a lot of people it can be a real process of loss".* (Esa, 2002). Consequently, food memories hold both sense of Loss and Joy.

The ''process of Loss'' is involved in Serine's questioning of the Italian waiter Eustavio if "he think immigrants are sadder than other people? He replies, ''Sadness? Certo! when we leave our home we fall in love with our sadness'' (Jaber, Crescent , 2004). Moreover, Serine's uncle tackles the notion of Sadness and loneliness of immigrants. The uncle states that "talking about the difference between then and now, and what's often a sad thing. And immigrants are always a bit sad right from the start any ways'' (Jaber, Crescent , 2004).One reason for the existence of sadness is that one cannot go back; "The Iraq your father and I came from doesn't exist anymore, that makes things sadder in general'' (Jaber, Crescent , 2004). At the same time that they converse, Serine makes a dessert. ''It melts into a dozen separate flavors. She can smell oranges and lemons, cherry and wood, and even the soft silk and wool of Persian carpets, the smell she thought came from Iraq'' (Jaber, Crescent , 2004). Remembering her child experience as she was shopping for food with her uncle, Serine epigraphs that:

"it didn't matter if the shop was Persian, Greek, or Italian, because all of them had the same great bins of beans and lentils, glass cases of white cheeses and braided cheeses, murky jars of olives, fresh breads and pastries flavoring the air" (Jaber, Crescent , 2004)

In this context, food seems to be a universal item that has common denominators: olives, garlic, Lentils, and other foods; which can be used in middle-eastern cooking and also be the basement ingredients in cooking of other cultures. Here, It is of paramount importance to deal with the notion of food migration as well as the migration of identity. This explains the illusory nature of borders and nationality. Bhabha and Appiah argue that culture is not static, but is in mobility:

"But trying to find some primordially authentic culture can be like peeling a onion… cultures are made of continuity and changes and the identity of a society can survive through these changes" (Appiah, 2006) .

Appiah notes that "most of those who have learned the languages and customs of other places haven't done so out of mere curiosity. A few were looking for food, for thought; most were looking for food" (Appiah, 2006).

The cross-cultural pollination that Appiah described ironically as a "contamination" has been operating in Markets and kitchens for centuries around the world. Thus, food can be mobilized as well as cooking can be politicized. This notion is marked out in *Crescent* as celebrating the thanks giving. Metaphorically speaking, Serine prepares an "Orphan" thanks giving, because it seems to be an assorted collection of unrelated friends. The concept of hybridity is sensed through the celebration of this feast which may be the most celebrated food in American holidays. This hybrid holiday is what Um- Nadia calls the ''old time Arabs' cooking''; say it contrarily; Diana uses food in order to make the reader aware of the complexity relationship between the guests. In the middle of concocting the thanks giving, Serine ''looked up Iraqi dishes, trying to find the childhood foods that she'd heard Han Speak of, the *sfeehas*-savory pries stuffed with meat and spinach-and round *mensaf* trays piled with Lamb and rice and yogurt sauce''. Whereas stuffing the turkey of breadcrumbs and giblets, Serine uses ''rice, onions, cinnamon, and ground Lamb'' (Jaber, Crescent , 2004). Moreover, traditional dishes are cooked.

The guests are contributing in preparation of the feast that hold ''a big round *fatayer*- a lamb pie- that Aziz bought from the green-eyed girl at the Iranian bakery; six sliced cylinders of cranberry sauce from um- Nadia; whole roasted walnuts in chili sauce from Cristobal''. Additionally, victor Hernandez, the bus boy from the cafe, "brought three homemade pumpkin pies and half-gallon of whipping cream'' (Jaber, Crescent , 2004). From this epigraph, which principally discuss the items of hybridity, cross-culturalism and the universality of food especially in celebrating the thanks giving. This multi- dimensionality of food embodies and represents home within this dinner, the guests discuss politics, food and they raise the questions about identity. What does it mean to be American? To be in America? Moreover, they debate the US punishments on Iraq and how it reflects badly on the society; spread of starvation, crime, and prostitution. Broadly speaking, political events can be related to cultural practices as Aziz inquires the guests to "Consider the difference between the first and third person in poetry''. Also, he states that "the difference between looking at a person and looking at that person, but lasting a piece of bread that they baked is like looking out of their eyes''. Aziz requires that '' you've got the soul of a poet! Cooking and tasting is a metaphor for seeing your cooking reveals America to us non- Americans and vice versa''. (Jaber, Crescent , 2004)

Appiah's idea of cosmopolitanism is taken into discussion through the thanks-giving dinner, as he states "cosmopolitanism shouldn't be seen as some exalted attainment, it begins with the simple idea that in the human community, as in national communities, we need to develop habits of coexistence: conversation in its older meaning, of living together, association'' (Appiah, 2006)

The thanks-giving highlights the coexistence notion and the building of community through conversation. Appiah also asserts that "conversations across boundaries can be fraught, all the more so as the world grows smaller and the stakes grow larger. It's therefore worth remembering that they can also be a pleasure'' (Appiah, 2006). The verities of food ways that Serine uses exemplify the idea of cultural contamination of Appiah's theory of cosmopolitanism. In an ironical way, Serine deals with idea of cross-culturalism even if she is never being outside Los Angles. Serine utilizes the act of cooking to shed light on her cultural roots and mix old with new, past with present, the personal with political. The thanks giving dinner seems to stands as feast where a mixture of dishes bump up against each other and the finding of cranberry jelly everywhere all whose sits upon a table of middle Eastern food and pumpkin pies. This scene let Serine's uncle to exclaim, '' Well, look at us'': setting around here like a bunch of Americans without crazy turkey. All right now, I want to make a big toast here's to sweet, unusual families, pleasant dogs who behave, food of this nature, the seven types of smiles, the crescent moon, and a nice cup of tea with mint everyday Sahtain. Good luck and God bless everyone. (Jaber, Crescent , 2004).

As result, the thanks-giving banquet seems to be a theme that symbolizes the cross-cultural issue in the novel *Crescent*. Why? Because of the dinner which represents and gives the sense of home'' and this Summon the gathering of guests around the table. Thus, the generosity of community that gathers to cook, eat and share their stories reduced the losses of suffering caused by death and exile.

To conclude, the multitude of stories and histories in the novel are a hint of the complexity of identity and indicates that building a global community which perhaps starts from the kitchen. Abu Jaber asserts that food is "one of the most immediate and powerful ways of creating the metaphor of hearth and a gathering place, a place where the collective forms". (Esa, 2002) From this point, to build a community is to start from sharing meals and the conversation about small details in life. Moreover, through listening and believing in the power of storytelling, people put into existence a vision that brings hope for the future.

Bibliography

Appiah, K. A. (2006). *Cosmopilitanism: Ethics in a world of Strangers.* New York: Norton.

Bhabha, H. (1994). *the location of culture.* New York: Routledge.

Esa, A. S. (2002). Diana Abu Jaber: The only response to Silencing...is to keep speaking. *Aljadid: a review and Record of Arab Culture and Arts* , 8.39.

Fanon, F. (1967). *Black skin, White Masks.* New York: Grove.

Jaber, D. A. (2004). *Crescent* . New York: Norton.

Jaber, D. A. (2005). *The Language of Baklava.* New York: Pantheon.

Korsmeyer, C. (1999). *Making sense of Taste: Food and Philosophy.* Ithaca: Cornell UP.

Majaj, S. L. (1996). *Arab American Literature and the Politics of Memory.* Boston: Northeastren UP.

Pratt, M. L. (1992). *Imperial eyes: Travel Writing and Transculturation.* New York: Routledge.

Ratt, M. L. (1996). *food and identity.* londre: cambridge.

Shihab, N. N. (1995). *Words under the Words.* Portland: Eighth Mountain.

YOUR KNOWLEDGE HAS VALUE

- We will publish your bachelor's and master's thesis, essays and papers

- Your own eBook and book - sold worldwide in all relevant shops

- Earn money with each sale

Upload your text at www.GRIN.com
and publish for free